W9-AUO-718

THIS CANDLEWICK BOOK BELONGS TO:

_____

_____

_____

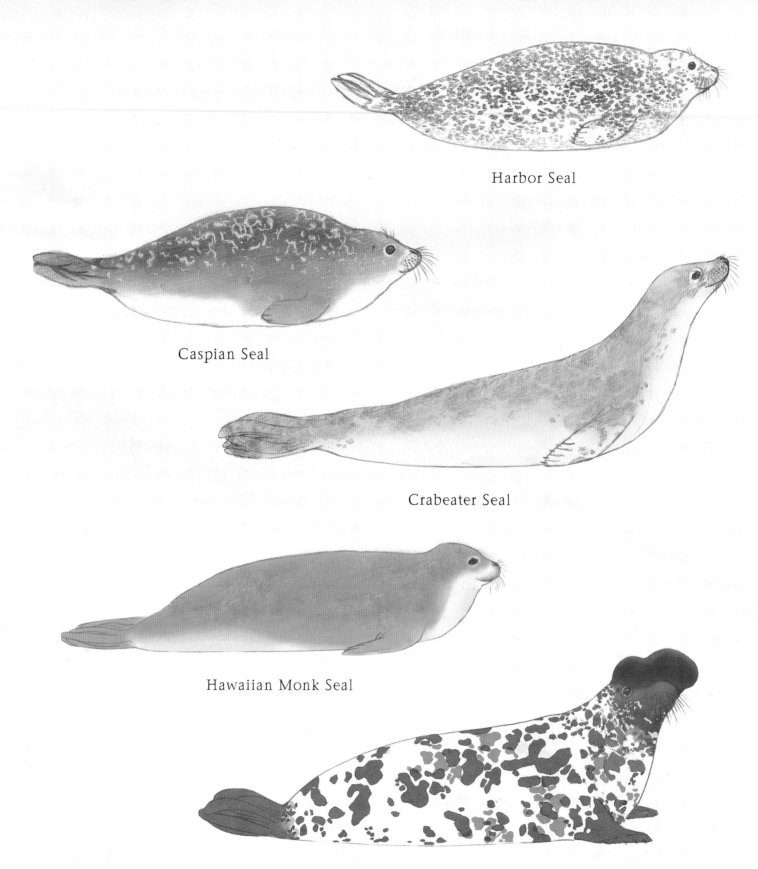

Harbor Seal

Caspian Seal

Crabeater Seal

Hawaiian Monk Seal

Hooded Seal

Gray Seal

Bearded Seal

Harp Seal

Baikal Seal

Northern Elephant Seal

For the Cornwall Seal Group
www.cornwallsealgroup.co.uk
C. B.

For my family
K. N.

The author and publisher would like to thank Sue Sayer, founding member of the Cornwall Seal Group,
for her invaluable advice and feedback during the preparation of this book.

WILD SEALS

Seals are sea mammals—but unlike dolphins or whales, they live partly on land, coming ashore to sleep, digest their food, molt their fur, and pup. You might even see wild seals if you're out walking by the ocean. Seals are curious and often look as interested to see you as you are to see them. It's wise to keep your distance, though, for your own safety, as well as the seals'.

You might see a fur seal, a sea lion, or a true seal. There are lots of differences between them—for example, fur seals and sea lions have ears you can see and long front flippers they can lift themselves up on, while true seals have short front flippers and ears you can't see.

This story is about gray seals—one kind of true seal. There are eighteen different kinds of true seals altogether—you can see pictures of them at either end of the book.

Gray seals used to be hunted, until they almost died out. Now they are protected by law in many countries around the North Atlantic Ocean, where they live. Their numbers have grown, though there are still not as many as there once were.

See What a Seal Can Do

CHRIS BUTTERWORTH

illustrated by

KATE NELMS

CANDLEWICK PRESS

IF you're down by
the sea one day,
you might spot a seal,
lying around like a fat sunbather
or flumping along the sand.

(A flump is a flop and a jump both together:
it's how a seal gets about on dry land.
It's not stylish, but it works!)

*The seals in this book
are gray seals, sometimes
called horsehead seals,
because of their long noses.*

*Seals are mammals, like us.
They are warm-blooded
and breathe air.*

And you might think
a seal's just a slow, dozy creature
that spends its time lazing around.

But you'd be wrong!

Seal spends most of his time in the sea;
it's where he finds all his food.

Gray seals mainly eat fish that live near the ocean floor, including Atlantic cod and sand eels.

He's off to look for some now. . . .

Seals spend time together in groups on land, but they usually swim alone.

Splash!

A big breath out
and down he goes.
His body's just the right shape
to shoot through the water:
sleek, smooth, and pointed at both ends.

*When you dive, you have
to take a big breath in—
but a seal blows
its breath out.*

His back flippers
power him
one hundred feet
down in seconds.

*Seals push themselves
through the water
with their strong back
flippers and steer with
their front flippers
and their tails.*

Seal slips through the seaweed forest—
big eyes searching the gloom.

His sharp ears hear dolphins
whistle and a ferryboat's
engine chugging.

Gray seals' ears are
just tiny holes behind
their eyes, yet they can
hear well underwater
and on land.

Seal's not the only
hungry one down here:
bigger things than him
are looking for their supper.

His long whiskers are his feelers:
they twitch as a silent swirl of water
tells him there's a killer whale
on the hunt for
a plump seal meal.

With a flick
and a twist of his flippers,
he dives deeper.

Only something
bigger and faster
than a seal
can catch it:
sharks and
killer whales
eat them.

Two hundred feet down, and it's colder,
but Seal doesn't mind.

He has two fur coats that keep
him waterproof,
and a thick layer of fat under his skin
wraps around him like a blanket.

Inside his blubber, Seal's
as warm as you and me!

*Gray seals molt, or shed,
their fur every year, which
keeps their coats thick
and waterproof.*

Gray seals live only in the
cool North Atlantic Ocean,
so they need to be able
to keep warm.

*Gray seals
can slow their
heartbeats to use
less oxygen. It helps them dive
deeper and stay down for longer.*

Three hundred feet down now, and
his heart gets slower . . . and slower . . .
until it only beats four times a minute.

Seal finds most of his food down here.
He swallows a few sand eels and
waits to see what else
might turn up.

At last, even gray seals run out of oxygen and have to come up for air.

But he can't stay
this deep forever.

Up he swims,
whiskers twitching,
ears sharp,
eyes wide—
and spies some
stragglers on
the edge of a
mackerel shoal.

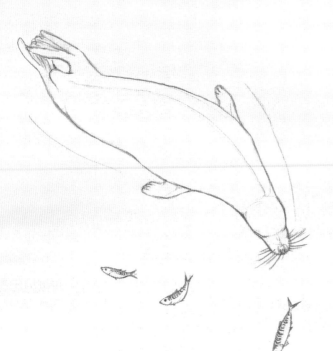

Then all at once,
with a twist

and
a turn,
he's on them.

Gray seals
eat some
fish from
nearer
the surface,
too.

Got one!

When gray seals
open their mouths
to catch fish,
their throats close
so they won't
swallow water.

Pop!

It's been a whole quarter of an hour since Seal's last breath of fresh air.

Seals can bend like bananas to keep their noses out of chilly sea water.

Back at the seal beach,
he's too tired to play with the others.

He finds a warm rock,
yawns,
stretches,
has a good scratch . . .

*Gray seals have five claws on
each front flipper — just
right for scratching!*

and falls sound asleep—as still
as his rock, but snoring loudly.

zzZZZZ!

So if you're down by the sea
one day, you might spot a seal,
lying around like a fat sunbather.

And you might think he's just a slow,
dozy creature that spends his time
lazing around . . .

but you'd be wrong!

Seal can dive like a rocket
and twist like a dancer—
he's a super-swimming
underwater wonder!

INDEX

Look up the pages to find out about all these seal things.
Don't forget to look at both kinds of words—**this kind** and *this kind*.

If you'd like to find out more about wild seals, here are some websites you could go to:
www.bbc.co.uk/nature   animals.nationalgeographic.com

Text copyright © 2013 by Chris Butterworth. Illustrations copyright © 2013 by Kate Nelms. All rights reserved. No part of this book may be reproduced, transmitted, or stored in an information retrieval system in any form or by any means, graphic, electronic, or mechanical, including photocopying, taping, and recording, without prior written permission from the publisher. First U.S. paperback edition 2015. Library of Congress Catalog Card Number 2012947729. ISBN 978-0-7636-6574-6 (hardcover). ISBN 978-0-7636-7649-0 (paperback). This book was typeset in Godlike. The illustrations were done in mixed media. Candlewick Press, 99 Dover Street, Somerville, Massachusetts 02144. visit us at www.candlewick.com.
Printed in Humen, Dongguan, China. 19 APS 10 9 8 7 6 5

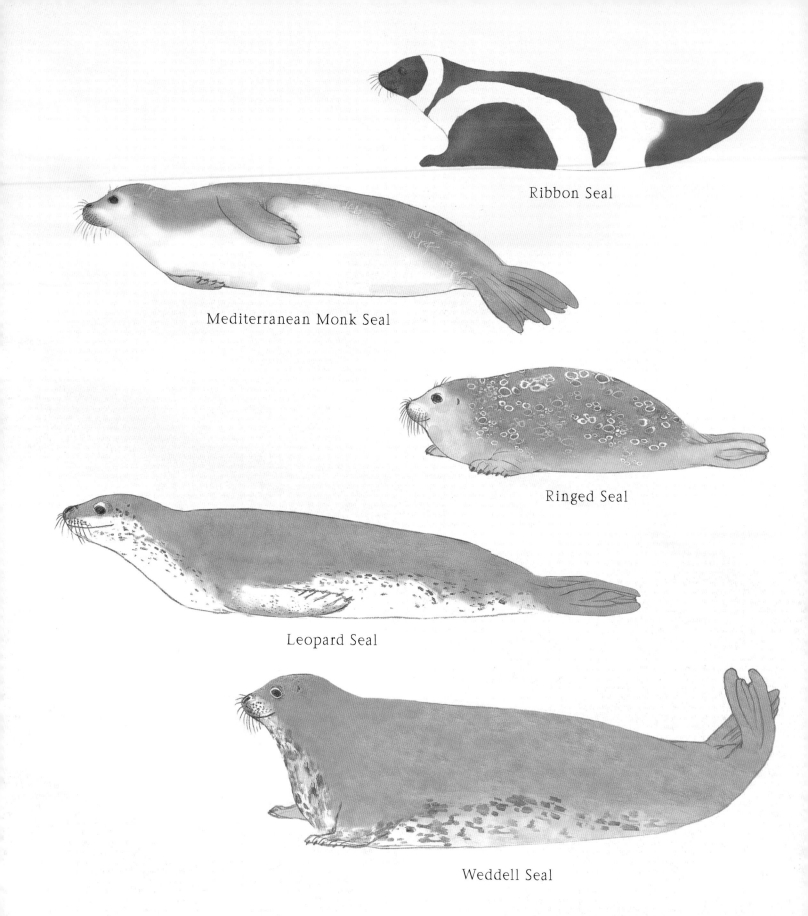

Ribbon Seal

Mediterranean Monk Seal

Ringed Seal

Leopard Seal

Weddell Seal

Ross Seal

Southern Elephant Seal

Spotted Seal

Chris Butterworth is the author of more than seventy nonfiction books for children, including *Sea Horse: The Shyest Fish in the Sea* and *How Did That Get in My Lunchbox? The Story of Food.* About *See What a Seal Can Do,* she says, "Whenever I'm swimming and I see a seal watching me, I feel privileged to be able to share its bit of the sea. It's good to be able to return the favor by letting readers know what attractive creatures they are." Chris Butterworth lives in England.

Kate Nelms graduated from the University of the West of England in 2010 with a BA in illustration. *See What a Seal Can Do* is her first book, and she says, "With such an expressive (and sometimes silly) face and wonderfully inquisitive personality, the gray seal is the perfect character to take you on a guided tour down to the watery depths of the North Atlantic Ocean in search of a meal." Kate Nelms lives in England.